T0199200

Last Days Psalms

Jean Schmeling

WestBow Press books may be ordered through booksellers or by contacting:

WestBow Press
A Division of Thomas Nelson & Zondervan
1663 Liberty Drive
Bloomington, IN 47403
www.westbowpress.com
1 (866) 928-1240

ISBN: 978-1-5127-2191-1 (sc)
ISBN: 978-1-5127-2192-8 (e)

Library of Congress Control Number: 2015919484

Print information available on the last page.

WestBow Press rev. date: 03/01/2016

WestBow
PRESS®
A DIVISION OF THOMAS NELSON
& ZONDERVAN

Table of Contents

The Last Days

Are we in the Last Days?

Save us from our evil ways.

The signs and wonders tell us the end is near.

If we receive Jesus, we need not fear.

    We must save souls.

    Heaven knows.

The Big Bang

The big bang was a fine-tuned design.
We believers knew it all the time.
There was a causal agent.
Scientists call God transcendent.

Awesome universe of divine design,
what the Bible tells us now proven.
Laws and distance and timing so fine,
glorious is God's creation.

Flash to darkness too hot before light,
fourteen billion years of chemical nebulae,
from baby stars to supernova halos so bright,
red and blue dance of life to make us sigh.

Low odds for a galaxy of spiral,
not the dense center or spatial,
just the right place for great viewing,
to study the divine tuning.

Our rare star just right in size and place.
for God's Garden of Eden in space.
Ashes of all the galaxies' supernova
for God's greatest creation in His image Adam.

What a time to be alive,
with God's design proven so fine.
Ten billion trillion stars
needed for life on earth. It's ours.

Glorious are God's Works

Glorious are God's works,
how awesome His universe,
how beautiful our earth,
to welcome us at birth.

Amazing creatures for our sight,
plants of colors and scents to delight,
lush fruit and music's melody,
majestic landscapes from sea to sea.

God is love, truth and beauty.
Your children give You glory.

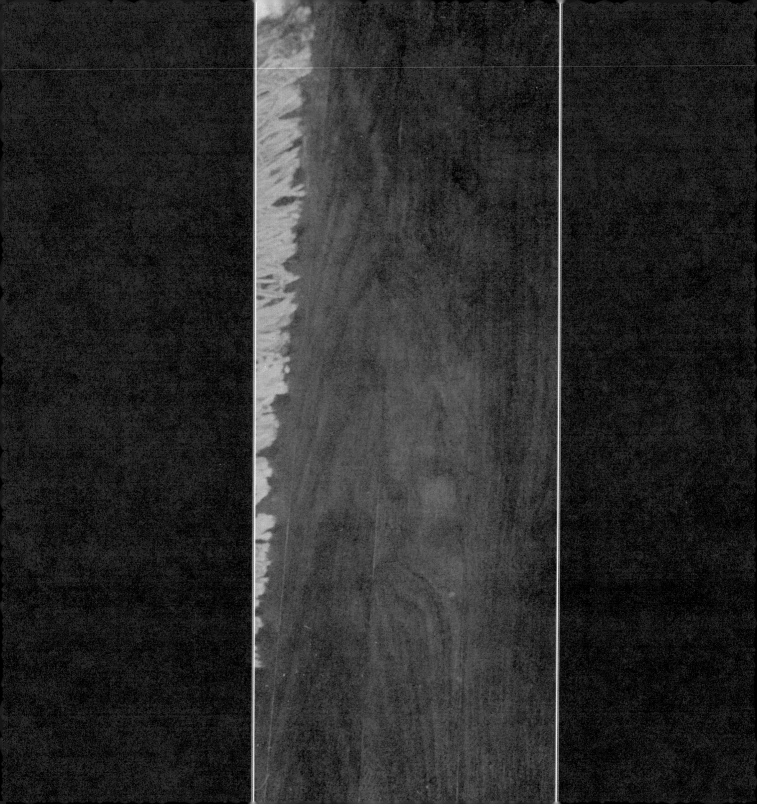

The Holy Trinity

I see the Holy Trinity
etched in my hard-wood floor.
What a blessing for me,
eternity to adore.

When I prayed that I would see God's face,
placing my hands on theirs on TV,
I happened to see the Trinity.
Was it always there waiting for me?
----for this time and place?

Interwoven on God's almighty face,
descends Jesus with moving hands of blessing.
On high is Jesus the Lord holding saints arriving.
His blessed mother prays at her place.

The Holy Spirit proclaims divinity.
What a perfect beautiful Trinity.
The pieta is seen through God's face
to save the human race.

ENTRÉE
ENTRANCE

OUR LIVES

How fast our lives fly by,
like a flash of lightening.
Do we ever understand why?
Is there more to life than living?

We struggle to survive the race.
We age like the changing seasons.
On a spinning blue ball, we find our place.
We keep our memories and learn the reasons.

The child of God stays in us and sees.
In our struggles we make our choices.
Fighting, screaming and crying, we hear voices.
By loving and giving, we receive God's mercies.

Where oh Where

Where oh where has goodness gone?
Where oh where can we be?
We are falling in the abyss.
Lost our way, Thy light we miss.

No God, no wrong or right.
Money is our might.
Taking life, serving flesh and greed,
not helping others in need.

Where oh where is our God?
Banished from our land.
With signs of warning,
we do not understand.

Where oh where?
Wrath or not?

Garden of Eden

We are destroying Your earth.
We are in need of rebirth.
We have not kept Eden Garden.
For this we ask Your pardon.

We have not followed Your commands.
War and famine in many lands.
It is like the time of Gomorrah,
immorality and euphoria.

To the time of the signs we're blind.
Do not send Your wrath on mankind.
Holy Spirit, guide us.
Oh Jesus, save us.

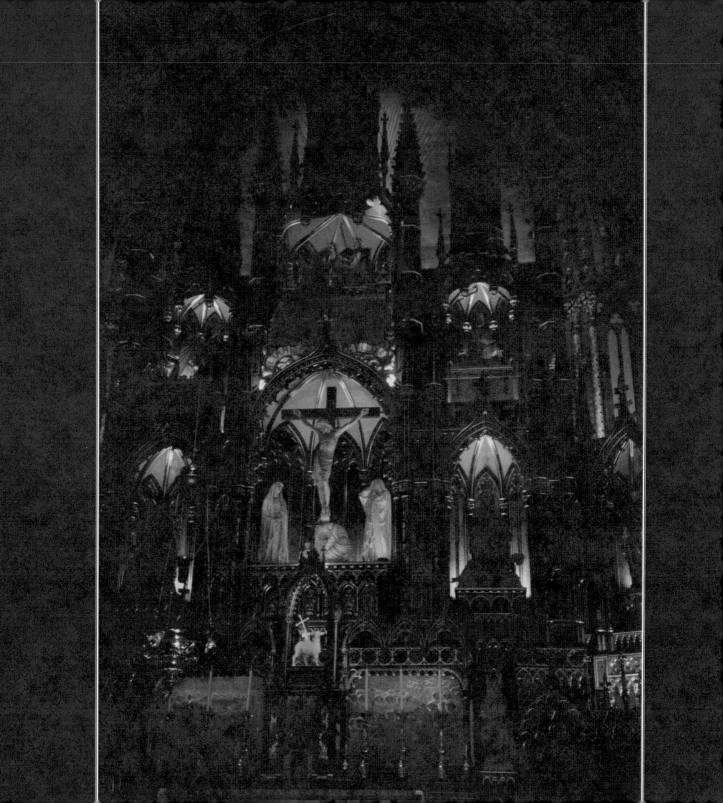

So Little Faith

We of so little faith,
we are afraid of these Last Days.
Iran and its uranium,
Moslem conquering heathen.

Destroying Israel is their evil plan.
Pestilence from animals in man.
We have not prospered Thy earth.
We're in need of rebirth.

Our Lord, give us faith.
Make our way straight.
Thou can make us safe.
Look up for our Savior.

Scary Times

These are scary times.
These are the time of the signs.
No respect, meek or strong.
No right, no more wrong.

Pestilence, epidemic strain,
weather extremes, too much rain.
Our earth is shaking.
Is this the awakening?

No jobs, house values going down.
No money, prices sky high.
No medical insurance.
So scarey to fly.

Wars abound—ethnic or power.
No more peace—terrorism.
Nuclear Holy War.
Rapture us, Jesus.

Nobody Cares

Nobody cares anymore.
Texting without compassion,
instant raw emotion.
What is it for?

Why can't we talk face to face?
Listening and showing caring eyes,
with respect, manner and grace?
Now nobody tries.

We've lost our heart and soul.
We don't hear God in constant chatter.
Programmed robots wanting to control.
What is the matter?

Out of Time

We're running out of time
in this human race.
Our world is imploding
into a black hole of waste.

Dying man on the street.
Passerby stares and leaves.
Violence in songs and video games.
No one to help or blame.

Medical care for greed not need.
Third world: no food, filthy water,
children for sex slavery.
Has the world gone crazy?
And lost its soul?

Haiti O Haiti

Haiti O Haiti
Awaken us from our greed.
Let us hasten to your great need.
Crushed beyond belief,
save us as your relief.

Haiti O Haiti
It is the U.S. in the dark.
We are under Satan's mark.
No longer God but flesh and greed.
The dignity of life is our need.

Haiti O Haiti
You are our trumpet call.
Touch our hearts in our fall.

Haiti O Haiti
Save us now.

The Judgment

Oh Lord, is this the time of the Judgment?
The wicked are sinking in the pit they made.
God sees all and will reward His children.
Nations that forget Jesus shall be afraid.

Let the earth shake and tremble,
raising waters that channel.
Moving foundations with fire and smoke,
as our God from heaven with thunder spoke.

The Lord will deliver the just,
to His fortress and high place.
For our faith God shall reward us.
The just will be saved to see His face.

Where Is America

Where is America in the End Times?
Are we to take the meteor's hit?
Why can't we see and believe all the signs?
We need to pray to God to forgive.

Prehistoric cultures predicted the date
for the shaking and devastation as earth's fate.
The Bible calls it the judgment and God's wrath.
Why can't Americans follow Jesus' path?

Look up for the Savior.
It's time to meet your maker.

Red Slime on the Tide

Red slime on the tide so wide.
Blue-green pristine Gulf sea.
Gooey toxic oil monster of greed
spreads ashore state to state stinky grime.

Sea life struggling to survive.
Oil plumes underneath the food chain.
Ruined refuges of wild life.
No way to stop, no one to blame.

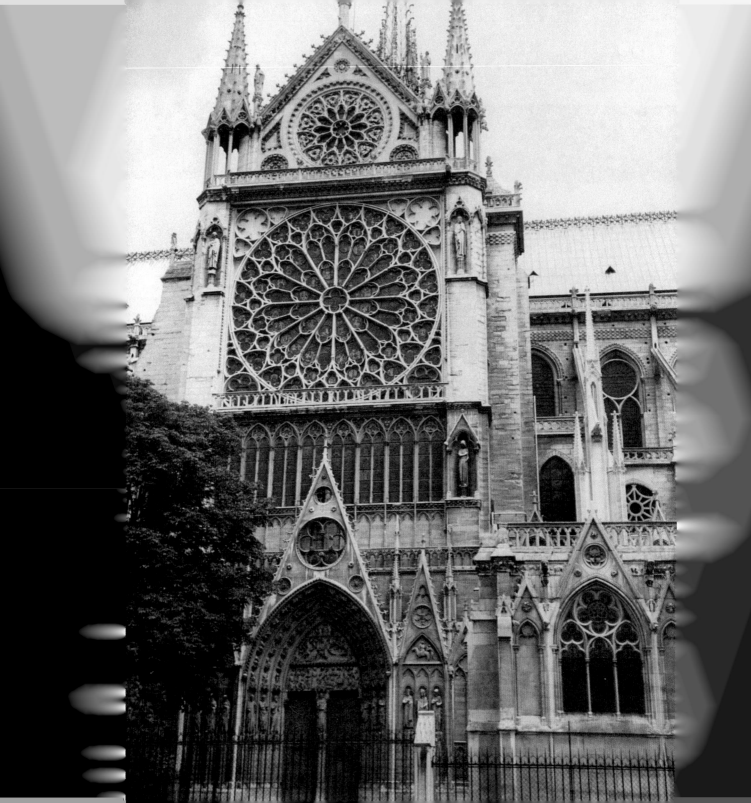

The Righteous

God trieth the righteous.
When will the end be near?
Lord, give me refuge from my fear.
I trust in Thy forgiveness.

Fly me to a safe place up high.
Hide me under Thy wing.
Jesus, save us as time draws nigh.
Praise to the Lord I shall sing.

Hallelujah
Peace be with you.

There Is Fear

There is fear upon the land,
trembling earth and economy,
famine, wars and disease.
The people don't understand.

God, we trust in Thee as our shield,
though ten thousand set up to terrorize.
We are like the lilies in the field.
From vanity we have turned our eyes.

Let Thy face shine upon us.
Thou maketh the sad become glad.
Surrendering all, we are the righteous.
We have safety, increase and Thy peace.

Prayers

Like incense prayers rise in the wind.
God hears and keeps what we pray.
We learn that love covers all sin.
The fire Spirit guides our way.

Why do we seek and keep treasure?
God's wisdom gives the greatest pleasure.
We learn to fear and wait in testing.
We dance for joy at our blessing.

What Will I Be

What will I be when I grow up?
When oh when will that be?
I want to keep the child in me.
I will sing alleluia.

His glorious wonders in verse:
the awesome universe,
the firmament of our earth,
the miracle of our birth.

Jesus told us so
so that we would know.
With praise I do receive.
In God and heaven I do believe.

Father Abba
Peace

Four-Leaf Clover

Four-leaf clover of my mother.
found in her psalms as my balm.
How she suffered at the loss of my brother.
My father's rage crushed her clover.

Now I carry the same cross,
a loving daughter lost.
I shall be like a tree by the water.
I thank God for the salvation of my daughter.

When I cried out to God in despair,
the Lord sustained me answering my prayer.
As His anointed, I shall sing His praise.
Thou, my God, will lift me all my days.

Sowing Tears

In our storms of life tears sow.
Look up for God's rainbow.
See our prayers in gold vials.
God, anoint us in our trials.

I cry out in my need
that God will bless me in deed.
Lead me to Thy space of joy.
Looking up I see God's glory.

Our Life is Just a Spark

Our life is just a spark.
Why must we go through the dark?
The tests and trials of life
bring us back to the light.

Why do our loved ones suffer and die?
If it is to be our cross,
how do we live with such a loss?

Is life a spiral of our choices?
Does God listen to our voices?
Yes, God sent me dreams and wonders.
Now I live to help others.

The Age of Grace

Is the age of grace near an end?
As the planets line up in place,
to rapture us Jesus will descend.
Holy Father, show us Your face.

It is the time to reach all the earth.
It is the time to spread the word.
We must save souls before it's too late,
before God's judgments are their fate.

Although darkness may surround, we see the light.
Grace will abound with miracles and signs.
The elders shall have dreams from above.
The youth shall bring alive Jesus' love.

One World

One world nation.
One world religion.
One world to save.
No God, no salvation.

Everyone to take the implant.
The U.S. already has it planned.
The beast will rule by six six six,
to blaspheme God and be worshipped.

World without end.
Time for Jesus to descend.
Our unending spiral of time
is entering the sublime.

My Blessing

When I cried out from the depth of despair,
God blessed me with dreams in His mercy.
The Holy Spirit guides my desire to share.
I trust in Jesus, who comforts me.

I guard my heart and keep God's commands
although His ways I do not understand.
With my mission I have hope and my life tree.
Angels shall protect and deliver me.

My Day of the Lord

Today is my day of the Lord.
Though I walked through the fire of testing,
Your signs answered my cries and foretold.
I thank You, God, for my blessing.

Angelbird wanting to come to me,
morning and eve pecking on my window.
My hurt white pelican returns to see.
Messengers from heaven I know.

Holy God exists outside time,
using time to encode the divine.
At ten years my mission this day.
Your mercy is my shield I pray.

LITTLE JEAN ANN

Little Jean Ann, honors and beauty queen,
wake up out of your dream state.
The time has come to go for your dream.

So many lives I have had.
As a girl such fun and so glad,
three little brothers and cousins many.
Serious student, to study in France for me.

Not much money—working I did go,
to pursue my career, a teacher I will be.
A fairy tale, a husband and a baby,
until tragedy I did know.

My brother so like me taken at twenty.
A husband crazy for trains losing money,
for five years much suppressed anger,
a split family and adventure.

Off to Houston, a new life for Renee and me,
sights and shows, sharing and caring.
While Renee at UT-Austin did study,
I re-entered the single life dancing.

Destiny brought Ed my Prince Charming,
to carry me off to his land of sun and sea.
Just fifteen years with my darling,
our life of travels and visits to family.

At the loss of my daughter Renee to comfort me,
miracle dreams and signs for my grief.
With two daggers piercing my heart,
I must write what I feel—so apart.

Little Jean Ann, honors and beauty queen,
wake up out of your dream state.
The time has come to go for your dream.

Printed in the United States
By Bookmasters